WHEN IS A PLANET NOT A PLANET?

THE STORY OF PLUTO

ELAINE SCOTT

CLARION BOOKS

New York

ACKNOWLEDGMENTS

Many people were very helpful as I worked on this book. In particular, I want to thank Antoinette Beiser, librarian at the Lowell Observatory, Dr. Mike Brown at the California Institute of Technology (Caltech), Jane Platt from the Jet Propulsion Laboratory (JPL), and Stephen Tellier of the Lunar and Planetary Institute for their patience with me and my questions.

Clarion Books
a Houghton Mifflin Company imprint
215 Park Avenue South, New York, NY 10003
Copyright © 2007 by Elaine Scott

The text was set in 16-point Sabon.

www.clarionbooks.com

Manufactured in China.

Library of Congress Cataloging-in-Publication Data
Scott, Elaine.
When is a planet not a planet? : the story of Pluto / by Elaine Scott
p. cm.
Includes bibliographical references and index.
ISBN: 978-0-618-89832-9
[1. Pluto (Dwarf planet)] I. Title.
QB701 .S36 2007   2006100684

ISBN-13: 978-0-618-89832-9   ISBN-10: 0-618-89832-8

WKT 10 9 8 7 6 5 4 3 2 1

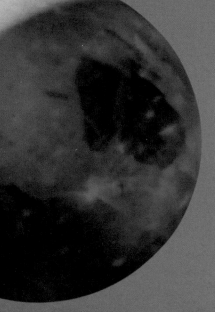

PHOTO CREDITS

Courtesy NASA/JPL-Caltech: 2, 22 • Peter Arnold, Inc./Alamy: 4 • Agence Images/ Alamy: 6 • Visual Arts Library (London)/Alamy: 7, 11 • Paul Almasy/CORBIS: 8 • Gustavo Tomsich/CORBIS: 9 • North Wind Picture Archives/Alamy: 10, 12 • Lunar and Planetary Institute: 16–17 (all planets) • Courtesy NASA/JPL-Caltech: 18 (Uranus), 19 (Neptune) • The Print Collector/Alamy: 18 (Herschel) • NASA, ESA, J. Parker (Southwest Research Institute), P. Thomas (Cornell University), L. McFadden (University of Maryland, College Park), and M. Mutchler and Z. Levay (STScI): 18 (Ceres) • Osservatorio Astronomico di Palermo: 18 (Piazzi) • Deutsches Museum: 19 (Galle) • NASA/JPL: 19 (asteroids) • NASA, ESA, and G. Bacon (STscI): 20 (Pluto) • The Lowell Observatory: 20 (Lowell, Tombaugh) • C. R. O'Dell (Rice University) and NASA: 24 • Michelle Gengaro-Kokmen: 25, 26 • Dr. R. Albrecht, ESA/ ESO Space Telescope European Coordinating Facility/NASA: 27 • Dan Durda, Fellow, International Association of Astronomical Artists: 28 • California Institute of Technology: 30 • Palomar Observatory, California Institute of Technology: 31 • Mark Garlick (Space-art): 32 • International Astronomical Union: 34 • NASA/JPL-Caltech/T. Pyle (SSC/Caltech): 35 • NASA: 37

CONTENTS

To my out-of-this-world friend, Diane Stanley

My very eager

mother just served us nine pizzas.

A silly sentence, yet schoolchildren have memorized it for

years, because it helps them remember the planets in our solar system.

The first letter of every word stands for a planet, in the order of how

close it is to the Sun. *My very eager mother just served us nine pizzas.*

Mercury, Venus, Earth, Mars, Jupiter, Saturn, Uranus, Neptune,

and Pluto. Mercury is the planet closest to the Sun,

and tiny Pluto is the farthest away.

That is, until recently.

Pluto is still there, of course. Along with the planets, aster-oids, comets, meteors, and bits of space rock and ice, Pluto is part of our solar system. Pluto and all those other objects orbit, or travel around, the Sun.

However, on August 24, 2006, the International Astronom-ical Union (IAU), a group of individual astronomers and astro-nomical societies from around the world, made an announcement. They declared that Pluto was not a planet. Suddenly, "My very eager mother just served us nine pizzas" didn't work anymore, because now there are only eight major planets orbiting the Sun. Perhaps someone will create a new sentence to help us remember their names and order.

Names are important, but they are not the only things to know about the planets. Learning how planets form, where they are located, and what they are like is the kind of activity that makes science exciting and fun.

My very eager mother just served us nine pizzas. This is a composite of photos taken on many different NASA missions. It illustrates our solar system. Our star, the Sun, is at the far left; Pluto is at the far right. The wispy tail of a comet is shown in the lower left, and the Southern Ring Nebula is near the lower right. The other faint objects in the image are artistic additions, created with a computer.

From the beginning of time, people have paid attention to objects in the night sky. Our ancient ancestors studied the Moon. They watched it grow from a tiny crescent-shaped sliver to a round ball of light, then slip back to a tiny sliver again. As they watched it, they began to mark off time. One full cycle of the Moon became one month. They noticed other things moving in the night sky—stars, comets, meteors, planets—which filled them with wonder and amazement. So they carved pictures of the planets, the Sun, the Moon, and stars onto rocks, and they painted pictures of them on the walls of their caves. These rock carvings and paintings still exist today. Some are over 20,000 years old.

The night sky has filled human beings with wonder and awe since the beginning of time.

Around 1000 B.C., the Greek people became very good astronomers—scientists who study matter in outer space. The Greeks noticed that some of the objects in the night sky were brighter than others. They noticed that these objects moved from east to west, across a background of stars that seemed to stay still. What were these things? The Greeks called them *planetes*—which, in their language, means "wanderers." Our word "planet" comes from that Greek word.

Why did the planets wander? In the ancient world, some people thought the planets were gods, walking across the heavens. Others, however, wanted a more scientific answer.

A bull, painted on the wall of a cave in Lascaux, France. Archaeologists believe the painting is 16,5000 years old and is an ancient sky map. The bull is part of the constellation Taurus, and the dots represent clusters of stars.

Ptolemy was one of the most important astronomers of his time. His theory that the Sun revolves around Earth lasted for 1,400 years. It is often called the *geocentric* theory; "geo" is Greek for Earth.

Ptolemy (TOLE-uh-me) was a Greek astronomer who lived from A.D. 100 to 179. He was one of the first to describe how planets "wander." Ptolemy said planets moved in an orbit, a curved path that one object travels along as it revolves around another. Anytime you run around and around something in a circle, you are orbiting it. Ptolemy believed that Earth was at the center of our universe, so he claimed that the planets, the stars, the Sun, and the Moon all orbited around Earth. For the next 1,400 years, people believed Ptolemy was right. But we know now that he was wrong.

A Polish astronomer, Nicolaus Copernicus (co-PER-ni-cus), came up with a different theory. Copernicus said it was the Sun, not Earth, that was at the center of our solar system. He said all the planets—including Earth—orbited the Sun. Copernicus lived from 1473 to 1543. During his lifetime, many people were afraid of his new ideas. Few accepted his theory about the Sun. A group of Christians who followed the teachings of Martin Luther and called themselves Lutherans were particularly upset with Copernicus. In fact, when Copernicus asked Andreas Osiander (oz-ee-AN-der) (1498–1552), who happened to be a Lutheran pastor, to publish his theories about Earth's orbit, Osiander changed the preface to the book! He wrote that Copernicus's ideas were just a *hypothesis,* a scientific prediction based on observations, not fact. But within a hundred years, things began to change.

In 1608, a Dutchman named Hans Lippershey (LIP-er-shy)(1570–1619) invented the telescope—by accident. Lippershey was an optician, someone who makes eyeglasses.

Copernicus's theory that the Sun is at the center of the solar system is called the *heliocentric* theory. "Helios" is Greek for Sun. Copernicus's ideas are so important they are often referred to as "the Copernican Revolution."

One afternoon, he was working with his lenses, and he held one in front of another. When he looked through both at the same time, Lippershey noticed that objects appeared larger and closer than they really were. Since it was difficult to hold the two lenses apart for any length of time, Lippershey put them on either end of a long tube . . . and the telescope was invented. At first, the new invention was called a spyglass. The Dutch military used it to look far out to sea, checking for any enemy ships that might be approaching Holland. However, when an Italian astronomer named Galileo Galilei (ga-luh-LAY-oh ga-luh-LAY-ee) got a spyglass of his own, he made improvements to it and looked up to the heavens, not out to sea.

Galileo's telescopes, mounted on a stand. Those who put Galileo on trial would not even look through them. In a letter to Johannes Kepler, Galileo wrote, "My dear Kepler, what would you say of the learned here, who . . . have steadfastly refused to cast a glance through the telescope? What shall we make of this? Shall we laugh, or shall we cry?"

Galileo, as he is known, lived from 1564 to 1642. Working with his telescope, Galileo discovered that Jupiter has moons orbiting it, just as our Moon orbits Earth. He also discovered that the Milky Way is not a smear of white in the night sky but is made up of individual stars—billions of them! Galileo agreed with Copernicus. He said the Sun was the center of our solar system, not Earth. However, many people were still not ready for new ideas. In fact, most people at the time thought Galileo's theories went against the stories in the Bible that seemed to put Earth at the center of the universe. In those days in Catholic countries like Italy, the church made the laws, and the church punished people who broke its laws. Galileo was put under house arrest. Others who agreed with him were punished, and some were even burned at the stake.

In 1663, the church found Galileo guilty of heresy for his beliefs. In 1992, the Vatican finally declared that Galileo's views were correct.

Fortunately, brave scientists continued to study the heavens anyway. At the same time that Galileo was working in Italy, Johannes Kepler (1571–1630) was working with a telescope in Germany. Kepler studied the sky through his telescope, and astronomy changed again. He became the first person to discover that the planets move in an elliptical, or oval, orbit around the Sun, not a circular one, as Copernicus and Galileo had thought. He also discovered that planets do not move at a steady speed. Instead, they move faster the closer their orbits take them to the Sun. Another of Kepler's important discoveries was that the time required for a planet to complete its orbit depends on its distance from the Sun. For example, Mercury, the planet closest to the Sun, completes its orbit around the Sun in 88 days. It takes Earth 365 days, or one year, to complete its orbit, while distant Pluto takes 248 Earth *years* to do the same thing. Kepler helped people understand *how* the planets move around the Sun, but no one understood *why* they moved. About forty years after Kepler died, an English mathematician named Isaac Newton answered that question.

Johannes Kepler, who was known for many scientific discoveries. Among other accomplishments, he was the first person to explain *how* a telescope works.

Isaac Newton not only discovered the law of gravity, he also worked with prisms to understand light, and he used a telescope to study the motions of the planets.

Few scientists try to solve a problem or answer a question from scratch. Instead, they build upon the work that scientists before them have done. Isaac Newton (1643–1727) understood Kepler's work, and it helped him make his own discoveries. Newton had been using a telescope to study the planets and their movements. One day, he watched an apple fall from a tree and began to think about the force that pulled it down. Since apples fall from the top branches of the tree as well as from those near the bottom, Newton realized that the force that pulled them down—gravity—reached all the way to the top of the apple tree. And if it reached the top of the tree, Newton began to wonder . . . could gravity reach all the way to the Moon? Using mathematics and observations made with his telescope, Isaac Newton hypothesized that the planets, stars, moons, asteroids, and comets—all the objects in the universe—have gravity, and that it is gravity that holds them in their orbits.

Kepler's laws had explained *how* the planets move. Now Newton's laws explained *why* they moved. Kepler's and Newton's discoveries formed the foundation for the study of physics. Physics is the science of how matter (anything that takes up space in the universe, whether it is solid, liquid, or gas) is affected by energy (the force that makes anything move, or work).

In science, when someone discovers a fact, or an event, that repeats itself over and over again, the discovery becomes a scientific law—something future scientists can rely upon to be true. Kepler's and Newton's discoveries are part of the laws of physics, and so far, these laws have never been broken. They are considered to be as true today as they were when the men discovered them. Scientists still use them as they conduct their investigations and gather new and exciting information about our universe.

3. IDEAS THAT WORK . . . AND THOSE THAT DON'T

Today, scientists do their work in much the same way that Kepler and Newton did. They begin with *observation*— carefully watching how something works. After some time of observation, they develop a *hypothesis,* which is a scientific explanation based on what they have observed. Using hypotheses, scientists can make predictions about what they expect to happen. For example, a researcher could have a hypothesis that a particular germ causes a disease. Or an expectation that a new planet can be found in a certain area of the night sky. A hypothesis is just an idea or an educated guess, until it is tested.

Scientists test their hypotheses over and over again. If the results don't disprove the hypothesis, they ask other scientists to test their hypotheses also. And if those tests produce identical results, the hypothesis becomes a *theory*. Scientists then begin to count on the theory being true.

You've probably developed theories of your own. For example, you may begin with an observation that the school cafeteria serves chocolate-chip cookies on Friday. From that observation, you might make the hypothesis that, on Fridays, the cafeteria will *always* have chocolate-chip cookies. If the cafeteria serves chocolate-chip cookies for six Fridays in a row, your hypothesis would appear to be correct. When more Fridays pass, and chocolate-chip cookies appear every time, you begin to operate on the theory that Friday is chocolate-chip-cookie day. If you were very confident, you would create your own cafeteria *law* that says Friday will always be chocolate-chip-cookie day. However, scientific theories—and even laws—can change if new information is discovered. If a

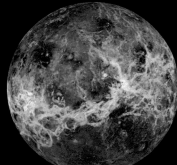

Mercury is one of the six planets known to the ancient world and is the planet closest to the Sun. After Pluto's demotion, it became the smallest planet in the solar system.

Ancient astronomers once called Venus the Morning Star and the Evening Star. After the Sun and the Moon, it is the brightest object in the night sky.

Planet Earth travels through space at 67,000 miles per hour as it orbits the Sun, which is 93.2 million miles away.

new cook starts working in the cafeteria and serves chocolate-chip cookies on Tuesday, your law would be broken, and your hypothesis and theory would have to change, too. Scientists must always be willing to abandon their theories when new information comes along that contradicts those theories.

Until 1781, everyone operated on the theory that Mercury, Venus, Earth, Mars, Jupiter, and Saturn were the only planets in our solar system.

Mars has been called the Red Planet since ancient times. On Mars, even the sky has a reddish tinge.

Jupiter is the largest planet in the solar system. If it were hollow, more than one thousand Earths could fit inside it.

Saturn has the most complex ring system of all the planets. It also has 31 satellites, or moons.

Then, in 1781, an English astronomer named William Herschel (1738–1822) discovered Uranus.

Twenty years later, on January 1, 1801, an Italian priest and astronomer, Giuseppe Piazzi (jo-SEP-ee pee-AHT-see), who lived from 1746 to 1826, was looking through his telescope. He saw a bright object—something new and different—traveling from east to west. It was large, about one-third the size of our Moon. Piazzi shared his discovery with other astronomers, and they determined Piazzi had found another new planet. It was named Ceres (SAIR-eez). But the following year, astronomers found an

Although they are not visible in this photograph, the Hubble Space Telescope revealed that Uranus has four major rings, and 17 known moons.

William Herschel discovered Uranus, but he had other scientific interests, too. In an experiment to see if colors had different levels of heat, Herschel tested his hypothesis by directing sunlight through a glass prism to create a spectrum. Then he measured the temperature of each color.

An actual photograph of Ceres, taken by the Hubble Space Telescope in January 2004. Unlike other asteroids, Ceres is round. It is approximately 600 miles in diameter, about one-quarter the size of our moon.

Astronomer Giuseppe Piazzi was a monk in Sicily and the founding director of the Palermo Astronomical Observatory. He discovered the first asteroid, Ceres.

object similar to Ceres in the same orbit. Then they found another. And another. The astronomers were puzzled. Could there be *that* many new planets? William Herschel suggested they give these small objects a new name: "asteroids." More and more asteroids were found. They were whizzing around in space, orbiting the Sun, just like Ceres. Astronomers named this region of space the Asteroid Belt.

Then in 1846, a German astronomer named Johann Gottfried Galle (GOL-lee) (1812–1910) discovered Neptune. Now there were nine planets in the solar system.

Neptune is 3 billion miles from the Sun and its orbit takes 165 Earth years to complete. Neptune is the smallest of the solar system's gas giants.

Johann Galle was a staff member of the Berlin Observatory and had already discovered three comets when he first observed Neptune on September 23, 1846.

Planetary astronomers think asteroids are leftover rocky matter from the formation of our solar system. Unlike Ceres, most asteroids are the size of pebbles, though some can be much larger.

Before long, however, astronomers began to change their minds about Ceres. Though it was much larger than other bodies traveling in the Asteroid Belt, Ceres wasn't traveling by itself, in its own orbit, as each of the planets did. Ceres was traveling with the asteroids. Also, compared to the other planets, Ceres was very small! Astronomers finally decided that Ceres was an asteroid—one of the largest, but still an asteroid. So Ceres was demoted. And the solar system returned to eight planets.

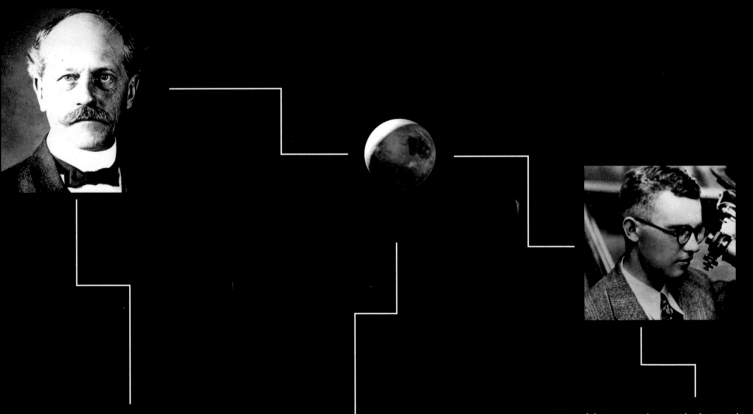

Percival Lowell had a lifelong interest in

An artist's conception of Pluto.

In addition to Pluto, Clyde Tombaugh also discovered 14 asteroids in the course of

Percival Lowell (1855–1916) was a successful American businessman, travel writer, and diplomat. He was not a professional astronomer, though he loved to study astronomy. In 1894, using his own money, he established the Lowell Observatory in Flagstaff, Arizona.

Lowell was fascinated with Mars, but he had another abiding interest. He hoped to find a ninth planet—one he called Planet X. As he studied the recently discovered Neptune, he noticed that the planet wobbled as it orbited. Using Newton's and Kepler's laws, Lowell decided that Neptune might be wobbling because the gravity of another, unseen, planet was tugging on it. He used the laws of physics to help pinpoint where this mysterious new Planet X might be found. Sadly, when Lowell died in 1916, he had still not found it. But in 1929, astronomers at the Lowell Observatory decided to look for Planet X again. A young astronomer, Clyde Tombaugh (1906–1997), used Percival Lowell's calculations to search the night skies. On February 18, 1930, he found what he was looking for—the smallest and farthest planet, Pluto.

But in time, there were problems with Pluto.

There are two groups of planets in our solar system. The planets closest to the Sun—Mercury, Venus, Earth, and Mars—have a solid surface made of a mix of rocks, dirt, and minerals. The planets farthest away from the Sun—Jupiter, Saturn, Uranus, and Neptune—don't have a solid surface. They are made up mostly of gas, with a rocky core. Scientists have a theory about why some planets are terrestrial, or made of rocks and dirt, and why some are composed primarily of gas.

Most scientists believe that our solar system is about 4.5 billion years old and that it all began as a space cloud, called a nebula. The nebula was made up of bits of space dust, rocks, ice, and gas. After 100,000 years or so, a tiny star, not yet ready to give light, began to form in the center of the nebula. The star was our Sun. Approximately 100 million years

An artist's conception of a protoplanetary disk forming around a star.

passed, and the hydrogen at the center of the Sun began to mix with another gas that was there—helium. When hydrogen mixes with helium, a nuclear reaction occurs, which releases energy. The Sun's release of this energy produces heat and light.

A small portion of the Orion Nebula, 1,500 light years away from Earth. At least 153 stars in this region have protoplanetary disks swirling around them, forming new solar systems. Scientists believe our solar system formed in just this way.

Meanwhile, the nebula continued to orbit the new Sun until it formed a large flat ring around it. Scientists call this ring a "protoplanetary disk." The disk, or ring, was hottest where it was closest to the Sun, and coolest at its outer edge. As the disk swirled around the Sun, the Sun's gravity went to work. It pulled and tugged at the bits of rock, dust, ice, and gas until they came together in clumps of material we now call the planets.

The planets that were closest to the Sun didn't keep much of their gas. The Sun's heat blasted it away, leaving behind solid spheres of matter, with only a little gas. Those spheres became the terrestrial planets—Mercury, Venus, Earth, and Mars. But on the outer edges of the disk, far away from the Sun's heat, it was much cooler. The clumps of rock and dirt there still had their thick layers of gas; they didn't burn away. The planets farthest from the Sun became the gas giants—Jupiter, Saturn, Uranus, and Neptune.

Because astronomers still believed this theory about how our planets formed, they had a problem with Pluto. When it was first discovered in 1930, astronomers assumed Pluto was made of ice and gas because of its great distance from the sun. However, by 1987, Pluto had moved into a position that only occurs twice in its 248-year orbit and scientific instruments had improved. Astronomers were able to study Pluto and the light that reflected off it. Their instruments told them that Pluto was dense and must have a rocky core. That new information raised questions. If the planets closest to the Sun were rocky and the planets farthest away from the Sun were mostly made of gas, why was Pluto—the most distant planet of all—made of rock?

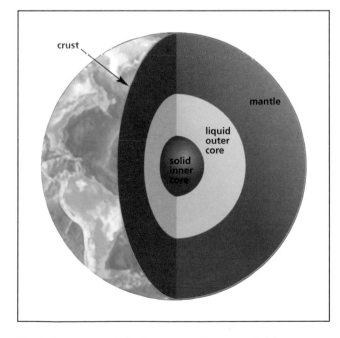

Earth is a terrestrial planet, which means it has a solid inner core.

Though they are made almost entirely of layers of gas, Jupiter and other gas giants have a small solid core.

Pluto's orbit

Neptune's orbit

All of the planets, comets, and asteroids in the solar system are in orbit around the Sun. Their orbits line up with each other, creating an imaginary flat disk called the orbital plane. Pluto's orbit, which takes 248 Earth years to complete, brings it outside the orbital plane. For 20 years of each orbit, Pluto moves inside the orbit of Neptune, making Neptune farther from the sun than Pluto. Pluto was inside Neptune's orbit from 1979 to 1999.

There were other questions as well. Pluto's orbit is different from the orbits of the planets. Think of an orbit as a lane on a racetrack. Just as runners have their own lanes on the track, each planet has its own orbit around the Sun. For the runners, all the lanes together make up the racetrack. For the planets, all their orbits, taken together, make up the "orbital plane." Just as runners don't run outside their individual lanes, planets don't travel around the Sun outside their individual orbits. Except for Pluto. Pluto crosses Neptune's orbit.

The shape of Pluto's orbit is different, too. The larger planets travel around the Sun in an oval-shaped orbit. Pluto's orbit is more of a stretched-out oblong. The other planets' orbits are level with the Sun. Pluto's is tilted. Comets' orbits are often tilted, so astronomers wondered, Could Pluto be a comet?

And of course there is Pluto's size. Astronomers knew Pluto was tiny when it was discovered in 1930. But because it was so far away, it was hard to see the planet clearly. Pluto appeared as a tiny dot of light in the night sky. Then telescopes improved. In 1976, American astronomer James Christy discovered that the tiny dot everyone thought was Pluto was really two objects: Pluto had a moon—Charon (CARE-en). Once astronomers discovered that Charon was separate from Pluto, they realized that Pluto was even smaller than they had originally thought. Pluto is only 1,440 miles in diameter. (Charon's diameter is 790 miles.) They began to ask, Is Pluto too small to be a planet? And since they had found Charon, they wondered, Were there more objects out there the size of Pluto? Were *they* planets, too?

Pluto and its moon, Charon. Pluto was 2.6 billion miles from Earth when the Hubble Space Telescope took this photo.

Objects in the Kuiper Belt are so far away,
it takes them hundreds of Earth years to orbit
the Sun.

5. FINDING PLANETS

In 1992, astronomers made an amazing discovery: 9.3 *billion* miles away from our sun is another region of space, shaped like a disk. Astronomers believe it contains approximately 70,000 icy objects, including Pluto.

This area of space was named the Kuiper Belt, after the Dutch-American astronomer Gerard Kuiper [KI-per] who lived from 1905 to 1973. In 1951, more than forty years before its discovery, Kuiper actually predicted that a region like this might exist.

Michael Brown, Chad Trujillo, and David Rabinowitz are planetary astronomers who study Kuiper Belt Objects, or KBOs. People often call these men "the Planet Finders." Together, they hunt for planets at the outer edges of our solar system using the Samuel Oschin Telescope at the Palomar Observatory in California. The Oschin telescope is a wide-field telescope, which means it views broad regions of the sky at once. When paired with a camera at the observatory, it can take pictures of these large areas.

In the past, astronomers had to spend their evenings peering through telescopes in order to study the night sky. Now things have changed. Robots control the Oschin telescope and its camera, and as Mike Brown has said, "I can actually have a wife and a life."

While Mike and the other astronomers are having their "life" in the evenings, the cameras in the telescope at the Palomar Observatory are at work. They take three photographs over three hours of the part of the night sky the men want to study. Any object moving across the background of billions of stars and galaxies will be captured in pictures. The pictures are then sent from the telescope's cameras to a bank of ten computers at the California Institute of Technology. Next, the computers decide which objects appear to be moving and

They call Mike Brown (*left*), Chad Trujillo (*center*), and David Rabinowitz (*right*) "the Planet Finders." Mike is pictured with the Oschin telescope, which the team used to discover Eris.

therefore might be a planet. Usually, the computers select about 100 objects; when the men arrive at work each morning, the pictures are ready for them to view.

Mike Brown says most of the objects he looks at on his computer screen are not planets. Many are caused by some kind of flaw in the telescope's camera. But every once in a while, an astronomer will get very lucky and something new and exciting will appear. That's how Mike and his team discovered 2003UB313, or Xena (ZEE-nah), as it was nicknamed, on October 21, 2003. Mike says, "The very first time I saw Xena on my screen, I thought that there was something wrong. It was too big and too bright. Then I did a calculation of how big it was and how far away it was. Xena is the most distant object ever seen in orbit around the Sun."

Pluto is 3.6 billion miles away, but Xena is 10 billion miles away and is approximately 400 miles bigger in diameter than Pluto. It takes Xena more than twice as long as Pluto to orbit the Sun.

Xena was always a nickname. On September 13, 2006, the newly discovered celestial body officially became Eris (AIR-is), for the Greek goddess of strife and discord. It seems an appropriate name, since there was a lot of strife and discord surrounding Eris. Was it a planet, or not?

The first images of Eris, taken at one-hour intervals on the night of October 21, 2003. Eris moved slowly across the night sky over the course of three hours.

An artist's conception of the Milky Way, our home galaxy. The
Milky Way is a spiral galaxy that contains 100 billion stars.

Because scientists always check and recheck their work, Mike Brown and his team of astronomers didn't announce their discovery of Eris until January 5, 2005, after they had had a chance to verify their information. When they revealed their discovery, many people thought the solar system had gained its tenth planet. But others disagreed. Soon an argument was raging among astronomers all over the world. And the argument came down to one question. What, exactly, is a planet?

It seems surprising, but until August 24, 2006, science had never had a definition for the word "planet." Dictionaries had definitions, of course, but most said something similar to "A large celestial body that circles around the Sun or another star." For a scientist, that definition had problems. For one thing, what is meant by "large body"? Jupiter, the largest planet in our solar system, is 88,700 miles in diameter, and it is a planet. Pluto is only 1,440 miles in diameter and—at the time—it was a planet, too. The question "What is a planet?" needed an answer, and the International Astronomical Union decided to create not one definition but three.

The IAU came up with three classes of objects that orbit the Sun: planets, dwarf planets, and small solar-system bodies.

The IAU decided that a celestial body is a planet if it:

1. orbits the Sun
2. is round or nearly round, because its gravity has pulled it into that shape
3. is big enough and has enough gravity to "clear the neighborhood" around its orbit

The first two qualifications for planethood, orbiting the Sun and a round shape, are easy to understand. The concept of "clearing the neighborhood" is a little more difficult.

The Planet Definition Committee.
Top row, from left:
Dr. Andre Brahic, France;
Dr. Iwan Williams, England;
Dr. Junichi Watanabe, Japan;
Dr. Richard Binzel, USA;
bottom row, from left:
Dr. Catherine Cesarsky, president-elect of the IAU;
Dava Sobel, author;
Dr. Owen Gingerich, USA.

It might help to think of planets as the schoolyard bullies of the solar system. In order to clear the neighborhood, a planet has to be big enough, and have enough gravity, to get rid of any celestial objects in its way. A large planet might clear its orbit by using its gravity to pull other, smaller, objects toward it and destroy them, the way asteroids are destroyed when they hit Earth.

A cosmic collision. Planets often "clear their neighborhoods" in this manner.

Or a planet might clear its orbit by attracting smaller objects toward it, then turning them into moons that remain in orbit around the planet.

Sometimes a planet will simply push a smaller body into a completely different orbit and get rid of it that way. But no matter how it does the clearing, according to the IAU definition, a planet must travel in its orbit by itself.

The second category of planets, called "dwarf planets," have the following characteristics. They must:

1. orbit the Sun
2. be round
3. not be a moon or satellite of any another planet

By this definition, Pluto is a dwarf planet. And although Charon, its former moon, is still locked in an orbit with Pluto, it is a dwarf planet, too. Now they are known as a double-planet system. Ceres is a dwarf planet, also, and Mike Brown's discovery, Eris, is one as well. They are dwarf planets because they orbit the Sun, they are round, and they are not moons of another planet—but they're too small to have enough gravity to clear their neighborhood. Pluto, Charon, Ceres, and Eris are all KBOs—orbiting far out in space with other objects in the Kuiper Belt.

Everything else—asteroids, comets, meteors—are now members of the third class of objects that orbit the Sun and are called "small solar-system bodies."

Some astronomers think the definition of a planet will change again in the future. Others think the current definition is a good one and will last.

Science is exciting, because it continually changes as new information is discovered. A long time ago, we thought there were six planets. Then we thought there were eight. For a while, with Ceres, there were nine. Then it was back to eight. Then, with Pluto, the number jumped up to nine again. And now it's back to eight. And that is just in *our* solar system!

We know our Sun is not the only star that has planets in orbit around it. New planets are forming around other stars, making new solar systems. There are 200 billion stars in the Milky Way galaxy alone. And there are billions of galaxies, full of stars, in the universe. As we study those planets and the stars they orbit, we ask questions. Are there other planets like Earth somewhere in the universe? Does life exist on them? We ask questions as we study the planets in our own solar system, too.

An artist's conception of the New Horizons spacecraft as it arrives at Pluto. Charon is visible in the distance.

Does life exist on one of them, or even one of their moons? Did life ever exist on any of them? Is Earth the only planet with life? Are we alone in the universe?

In January 2006, NASA launched the New Horizons mission to Pluto. If all goes well, the New Horizons spacecraft will reach Pluto and Charon sometime in the summer of 2015. Then instruments aboard the spaceship will begin to get a close look at these distant worlds. As the information beams back to Earth, scientists here will study it, trying to learn more about the origins of our solar system and what lies at its outer edges. Pluto still has a story to tell. There are questions that need answers, and the answers will come through science. New information is just waiting to be discovered.

asteroid: a small rocky object in the solar system that orbits the Sun. Asteroids are too small, and travel too fast, to be considered planets.

astronomer: someone who engages in the study of astronomy.

astronomy: the study of stars, planets, and other celestial bodies outside Earth's atmosphere.

celestial body: a naturally occurring object visible in the sky.

comet: a celestial body made of frozen dust and gas; comets often form long, bright tails.

dwarf planet: a celestial body that orbits the Sun and is not a moon or satellite of another planet. Unlike planets, a dwarf planet is not large enough to clear its orbit of other objects.

energy: the ability to do work; the ability to cause matter to move or change.

gas giant: a large planet, such as Jupiter, that is composed mostly of gaseous elements.

gravity: the force of attraction all bodies or masses in the universe possess; the larger the body, the more gravity it has.

helium: a gas that is lighter than air.

hydrogen: a light gas that burns easily; the most abundant element in the universe.

hypothesis: a proposed scientific explanation based on observation.

International Astronomical Union (IAU): an international group of astronomical societies that has the authority to name stars, planets, asteroids, and other celestial bodies.

law: in science, a general statement that describes regularly repeating facts or events.

matter: any substance in the universe that takes up space; matter can be liquid, solid, or gas.

Milky Way: the galaxy that is home to Earth's solar system.

moon: a natural satellite of a planet.

nuclear reaction: any reaction that involves a change in the nucleus of an atom, which is the smallest part of matter.

observatory: a building or location outfitted with telescopes and other equipment for watching celestial bodies.

orbit: the curved path one object takes as it revolves around another.

orbital plane: the imaginary plane in space on which all the planets orbit.

physics: the science that studies how matter is affected by energy.

planet: a large round celestial body that occupies its own orbit around a star.

protoplanetary disk: a disk of dust and gas that orbits a new star.

satellite: an object that orbits another object in space; satellites can be man-made or natural.

solar system: a star and the collection of celestial bodies that orbit it.

star: a celestial body that creates its own light by nuclear reaction.

telescope: an instrument that uses lenses, mirrors, and sometimes cameras to make distant objects appear larger and closer.

terrestrial planet: a planet having a rocky surface; Earth is a terrestrial planet.

theory: a statement based on a confirmed hypothesis.

universe: all existing things, including all matter and all energy, on Earth and in space.

FOR ADDITIONAL READING

BOOKS

Croswell, Ken. *Ten Worlds: Everything That Orbits the Sun*. Honesdale, Pa.: Boyds Mills, 2006.

Fleisher, Paul. *The Big Bang*. Minneapolis: Twenty-First Century Books, 2005.

Orr, Tamra. *The Telescope*. New York: Franklin Watts, 2005.

Steele, Philip. *Galileo: The Genius Who Faced the Inquisition*. Washington, D.C.: National Geographic, 2005.

Taylor-Butler, Christine. *Pluto*. New York: Children's Press, 2005.

Thomson, Sarah L. *Extreme Stars! Q&A*. New York: HarperCollins, 2006.

Wright, Kenneth. *Scholastic Atlas of Space*. New York: Scholastic, 2005.

WEBSITES OF INTEREST

National Aeronautics and Space Administration
http://www.nasa.gov
Explore the universe and learn about the latest discoveries.

New Horizons
http://pluto.jhuapl.edu
Launched on January 16, 2006, New Horizons is the first mission to Pluto and is scheduled to arrive at the edge of our solar system in 2015. The site includes mission information as well as educational materials for teachers and students.

Welcome to the Planets

http://pds.jpl.nasa.gov/planets/welcome/pluto.htm

The Jet Propulsion Laboratory of the California Institute of Technology hosts a collection of many of the best images from NASA's planetary exploration program with extensive annotations.

Star Child: A Learning Center for Young Astronomers

http://starchild.gsfc.nasa.gov/docs/StarChild/StarChild.html

The Astrophysics Science Division of NASA provides an interactive site, divided into two age-appropriate levels, offering information and educational activities related to space, astronomy, and the solar system.

Amazing Space

http://amazing-space.stsci.edu

Designed primarily for educators but available to everyone, this site offers answers to cosmic questions, homework help, images, and online explorations that encourage learning through interactive programs.

Home page of Michael E. Brown, Division of Geological and Planetary Sciences, California Institute of Technology

http://www.gps.caltech.edu/~mbrown

An informative and entertaining page that includes Mike's story of finding Eris and his reaction to Pluto's demotion.

Note: Page numbers in **bold** type refer to illustrations.